It's a good day, some people would say, to get a bit of good news!

But nobody won the lottery.

It didnt suddenly rain ice cream

And we aren't going on a cruise.

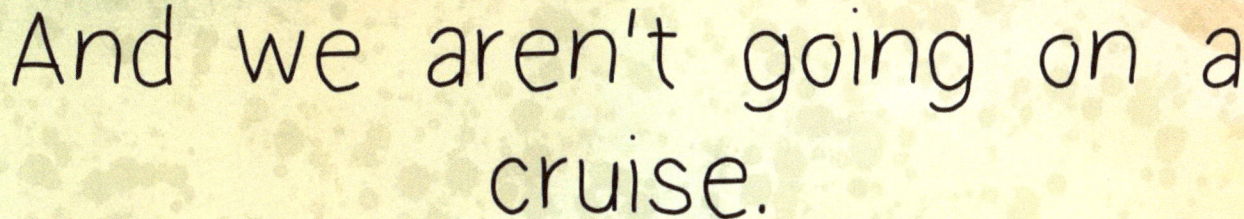

The police say speeding is still frowned upon.

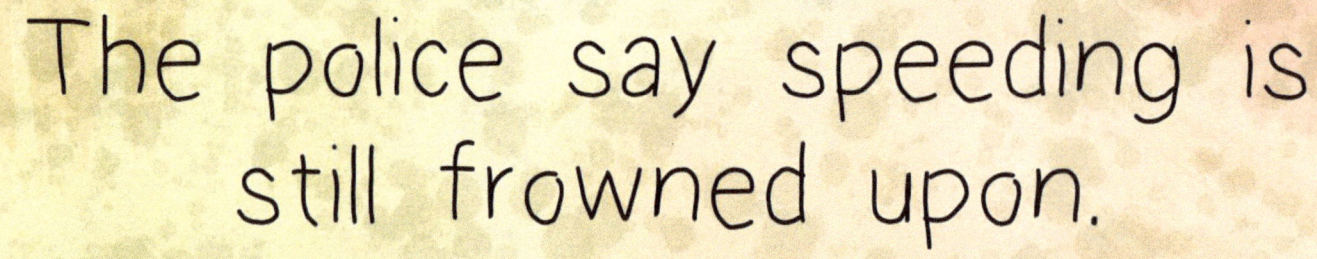

Our enemies didnt spontaneously combust

It's not a raise in your salary,

and sadly, our car in the driveway still has rust.

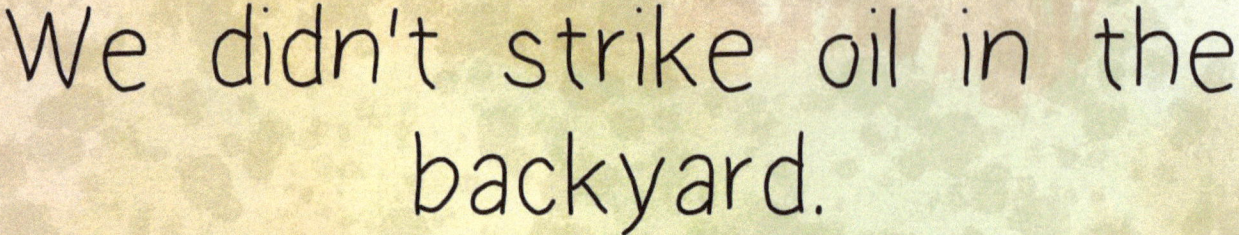

We didn't strike oil in the backyard.

It's not all-you-can-eat coupon at your favorite buffet.

It isn't a cool prize that you won at the fair,

but I guarantee that we'll look back fondly on this day!

The news isn't a whole banana split that you don't have to share!

It's not a new car from that game show last fall.

It's not a new puppy that's already trained.

It's not even a soft pretzel that you get at the mall!

I didn't find a diamond while digging in the garden.

All of the mosquitos haven't been sent into space.

No rich guy made us the beneficiaries of his will,

and we didnt win a trophy in that race.

We haven't found a chest of gold coins in the attic.

Gas will never be back to pennies a tank.

and there wasn't a positive mistake at the bank!

The good news could be that you caught a fish as big as a whale!

Or it could be a brand new TV!

Maybe it's that all of your pants fit just right,

and that chocolate is now calorie free!

It could be, that from now on, you will always get the best parking spot!
No really!
It could be!
But it's probably not.

OK! OK! I'll tell you. I'm quite enjoying this, as you can probably see.
I bet the suspense is killing you, because
I know it's killing me!

The best news you've ever heard could be on the next page!
If you are smart, you will read this news loudly and preferably on stage!

This truly is **THE BEST** news! Thats not a *Maybe*

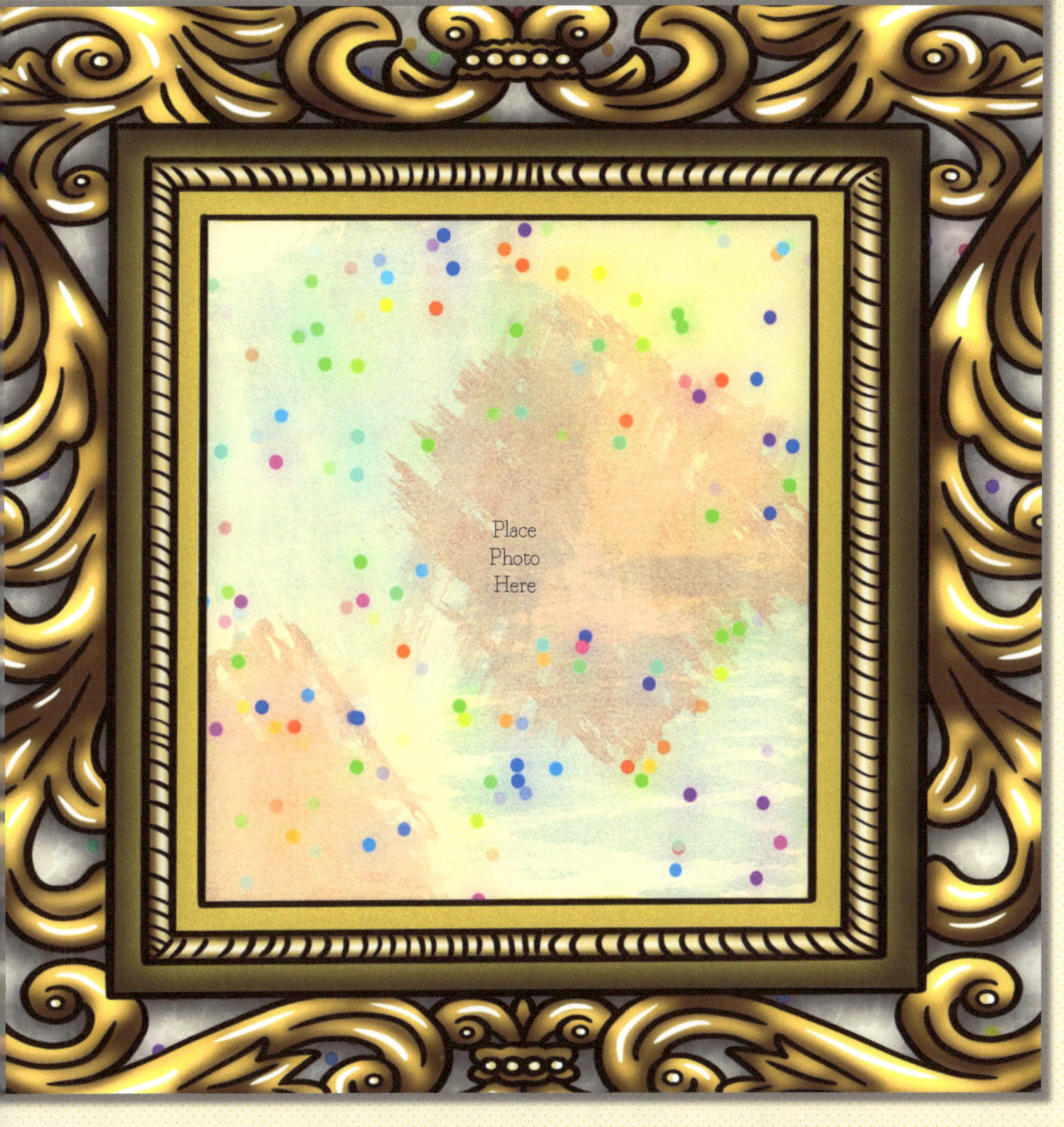

www.ingramcontent.com/pod-product-compliance
Lightning Source LLC
Chambersburg PA
CBHW061400090426
42743CB00002B/88